Strasbourg in the Dock

Strasbourg in the Dock:

Prisoner Voting, Human Rights & the Case for Democracy

Dominic Raab

Foreword
by
Lord Carlile of Berriew QC

Civitas: Institute for the Study of Civil Society
London

First Published April 2011

© Civitas 2011
55 Tufton Street
London SW1P 3QL

email: books@civitas.org.uk

ISBN 978-1-906837-21-1

Independence: Civitas: Institute for the Study of Civil
Society is a registered educational charity (No. 1085494)
and a company limited by guarantee (No. 04023541).
Civitas is financed from a variety of private sources to
avoid over-reliance on any single or small group of donors.

All publications are independently refereed. All the
Institute's publications seek to further its objective of
promoting the advancement of learning. The views
expressed are those of the authors, not of the Institute.

Typeset by
Civitas

Printed in Great Britain by

Berforts Group Ltd
Stevenage SG1 2BH

Contents

Author

Dominic Raab studied law at Oxford and Cambridge, where he won the Clive Parry Prize for International Law. He started his career as an international lawyer at Linklaters, working on project finance, international litigation and competition law. He also spent time on secondments at Liberty and in Brussels advising on EU and WTO law. In 2000 he joined the Foreign & Commonwealth Office where he advised on a wide range of briefs, including UK investor protection, maritime issues, counter-proliferation and counter-terrorism, the UK overseas territories and the international law of outer space. In 2003, he was posted to The Hague to head up a new team, focused on bringing war criminals—including Slobodan Milosevic, Radovan Karadzic and Charles Taylor—to justice. On return to London, he advised on the Arab-Israeli conflict, EU law and Gibraltar.

He left the FCO in 2006, and worked for three years as chief of staff to respective Shadow Home and Justice Secretaries, advising in the House of Commons on crime, policing, immigration, counter-terrorism, human rights and constitutional reform. On 6 May 2010, he was elected MP for Esher and Walton.

In January 2009, he published his first book, *The Assault on Liberty—What Went Wrong with Rights* (Fourth Estate), criticising the Labour government's approach to human rights and making the case for a British Bill of Rights. In October 2010, he followed this with *Fight Terror, Defend Freedom*, on the Home Office counter-terrorism review.

Dominic Raab has visited, studied and worked across Europe, the US, Latin America and Asia. He is particularly interested in the Middle East, having studied and worked in Israel and the West Bank, and travelled around Egypt and Pakistan. In 1998, he spent a summer at Birzeit University (near Ramallah), and worked for one of the principal Palestinian negotiators of the Oslo peace accords, assessing World Bank projects on the West Bank.

Nor is there liberty if the power of judging is not separate from legislative power... If it were joined to legislative power, the power over the life and liberty of the citizens would be arbitrary, for the judge would be legislator.

Montesquieu, *Spirit of the Laws*, 1748

Foreword

In this paper Dominic Raab MP raises some issues of fundamental constitutional importance. The prisoner voting issue has highlighted the disconnect between the European Court of Human Rights and the British courts, and with the UK Parliament. Above all, he demonstrates the importance of ensuring that the interpretation of the European Convention on Human Rights, or indeed any Charter of Rights applicable in the United Kingdom, should reflect UK standards of justice rather than inhibit them.

One of the important issues raised is that the Convention is now an old document, created at a different time in history and to reflect the needs, fears and worries of that time. Much has changed in Europe and in legal expectations during the past 60 years. All this is reflected in public opinion: there is alarming evidence that the public regards the Convention and its consequences as out of step with reasonable public expectation: law that does not command public respect is of understandable concern to politicians and the media alike. Perhaps the time has arrived for the Convention to be brought into the twenty-first century by a determined effort to modernise it?

Another key matter Mr Raab emphasises is the need for the Court of Human Rights to appoint judges of uniformly high calibre, with appointments to be founded on ability and skill in judgement, rather than national quotas.

A third and vital issue is about the margin of appreciation: the prisoners' voting issue is a clear example of a subject that may attract equally justifiable but markedly different conclusions in several countries. By its approach to this issue the Court of Human Rights has set itself on a collision course with our own jurisdiction, and with Parliament. The sovereignty of Parliament is not unqualified, but qualifications where they exist must be fully acceptable and gain the informed support of Parliament.

This pamphlet also deals with the vexed question of deportation of persons whose presence in the United Kingdom is found to be contrary to the public good and public safety. A narrow interpretation of the Convention has had a chilling effect on deportation, and thereby on public safety. This is an urgent matter, and Mr Raab provides forceful argument for a change in approach.

Whether the solutions Dominic Raab offers are adopted or not, he offers a cogent and well argued analysis, and interesting potential solutions.

Alex Carlile
Lord Carlile of Berriew QC

Summary

The ruling in *Hirst v United Kingdom* (2005) was a recent example of judicial legislation by the European Court of Human Rights (Strasbourg Court). There is no right to prisoner voting in the European Convention on Human Rights (ECHR). It was fabricated by judicial innovation, contrary to the express terms of the ECHR and the intentions of its architects, who specifically agreed to retain national restrictions on eligibility to vote.

The *Hirst* case joins a long list of examples of judicial legislation from the Strasbourg Court and, increasingly since the Human Rights Act 1998, the UK courts. One of the more serious examples is the expansion of human rights—especially the right to family life under Article 8 of the ECHR—to frustrate deportation orders. In one recent UK case, a man convicted of killing a young waiter from Esher avoided deportation, because the court ruled that the homicide offence was not serious enough to merit automatic deportation. The judge ruled that the perpetrator, an adult with no dependents, could claim the right to family life to trump the public interest in his deportation.

Senior members of the UK judiciary, including the President of the Supreme Court and the Lord Chief Justice, are expressing growing concern about the micromanagement of UK human rights law from Strasbourg. In addition to judicial concern, in February 2011, the House of Commons voted by a majority of over 200 to reject the *Hirst* ruling and retain the current ban on prisoner voting. In response, the Coalition government has indicated its intention to submit the *Hirst* ruling back to the Strasbourg Court for re-consideration.

The Strasbourg Court now risks triggering a con-stitutional crisis by attacking the will of the UK's elected law-makers, expressed through a 'free vote', in order to further its campaign towards the enfranchisement of all prisoners—a political rather than judicial agenda, that defies the terms of the ECHR and undermines the rule of law, the separation of powers and the basic principle of democratic accountability.

The government is right to challenge the *Hirst* ruling. It can refuse to implement the judgment without sanction or significant repercussions, such as being forced to pay compensation to prisoners.

However, the UK needs to pursue broader reforms to address the fundamental threat posed by judicial legislation. Whilst a UK Bill of Rights, to replace the Human Rights Act, could serve that end, such radical reform appears unlikely to command consensus amongst the Coalition parties in government. Therefore, in the short term, the Coalition should institute a series of bespoke reforms, tailored to strengthen the UK's democratic accountability and address the growing threat of expanding human rights law to Britain's ability to deport convicted criminals and terrorist suspects.

In particular, this report recommends that the government:

Amend the Human Rights Act 1998, in order to:

- **Enshrine free votes on Strasbourg rulings:** by amending the Human Rights Act to ensure that adverse Strasbourg rulings against the UK are subject to a debate in the House of Commons, coupled with a political commitment by the main parties to permit 'free votes'.

SUMMARY

- **Strengthen the independence of the Supreme Court:** by amending Section 2 of the Human Rights Act to check the wholesale importation of the Strasbourg case-law into the UK, strengthen respect for the common law and guarantee that the Supreme Court has the last word on the interpretation of ECHR rights as the UK's final court of appeal.

- **Defend the will of Parliament:** by amending Section 3 of the Human Rights Act, to prevent the courts from re-writing the express terms of legislation in order to pre-emptively avoid any inconsistency with the ECHR, where doing so would undermine the 'object and purpose' of the legislation according to the intentions of Parliament at the time of enactment. Section 6 should also be amended to prevent the courts from striking down the decisions of public bodies, where it would undermine the 'object and purpose' of the authorising legislation according to the intentions of Parliament at the time of enactment.

- **Remove fetters on deportation:** by amending the UK Borders Act 2007, deleting Section 33(2) to remove the express human rights exception and make a distinction between the bar on deportation to face torture or death and the bar on deportation that disrupts family life. This clause should be replaced by a specific regime for handling claims that a deportee may be tortured or killed on return home. In addition, the UK should avail itself of the 'margin of appreciation' to facilitate automatic deportation under the UK Borders Act 2007 for criminals convicted of serious offences and terrorist suspects, irrespective of claims that deportation would disrupt their family ties.

Pursue reform of the Strasbourg Court with the UK's European partners, through an amending Protocol that would:

- **Amend the Convention regime for deportation:** to create a specific regime to cover deportation, that reflects the distinctions drawn by the United Nations Convention Against Torture 1984. The UN Convention bars deportation to face torture but not lesser forms of mistreatment. The amendments should also clarify and confirm the express intention of the architects of the ECHR, that deportation on security or law enforcement grounds is not barred by claims of the right to family life under Article 8 of the ECHR.

- **Focus Strasbourg on the most serious human rights abuses:** by setting criteria whereby the Strasbourg Court only intervenes to hear claims that amount to the most serious or systemic violations of rights under the ECHR.

- **Introduce judicial quality control:** by tightening the procedure and criteria for judicial nomination and appointment, and increasing transparency and accountability over the process.

Avoid the 'triplication' of judicial legislation through developments at the EU, and in particular:

- **Ensure EU accession to the ECHR does not increase the liabilities of the British taxpayer,** by refusing to agree the terms of accession without further guarantees that it will not give the European Court of Justice in Luxembourg jurisdiction over the application of human rights in or by the UK.

Prisoner Voting— the Background to *Hirst*

The Hirst Case—a divided court

In 1980, John Hirst was convicted of manslaughter and sentenced to 15 years imprisonment for killing his land-lady with an axe when she pestered him to pay the rent. He served ten years more than his original sentence due to offences committed in prison, and was released in 2004. Hirst sued the government under the Human Rights Act 1998. He claimed the denial of his right to vote under UK law violated Article 3 of Protocol 1 to the European Convention on Human Rights (ECHR).

Article 3 of Protocol 1 provides a 'Right to Free Elections':

> The High Contracting Parties undertake to hold free elections at reasonable intervals by secret ballot, under conditions which will ensure the free expression of the opinion of the people in the choice of the legislature.

The High Court dismissed Hirst's claim, ruling that the UK's position on prisoner voting 'is plainly a matter for Parliament not for the courts'.[1]

Hirst took his case to the Strasbourg Court. In October 2005, the majority of the Grand Chamber of the Stras-bourg Court held by 12 to 5 that UK law violated Article

---

[1]   Paragraph 41, *Hirst -v- Attorney General*, [2001] EWHC Admin 239.

3, because it was 'disproportionate' to any legitimate criminal justice aim.

The Strasbourg Court made three principal arguments. First, the majority observed that: 'in sentencing the criminal courts in England and Wales make no reference to disenfranchisement and it is not apparent, beyond the fact that a court considered it appropriate to impose a sentence of imprisonment, that there is any direct link between the facts of any individual case and the removal of the right to vote'.[2]

Second, the majority argued that: 'there is no evidence that Parliament has ever sought to weigh the competing interests or to assess the proportionality of a blanket ban on the right of a convicted prisoner to vote... [i]t cannot be said that there was any substantive debate by members of the legislature on the continued justification in light of modern day penal policy and of current human rights standards for maintaining such a general restriction on the right of prisoners to vote'.[3]

Third, the majority held that the ban on prisoner voting under the relevant UK legislation, Section 3 of the Representation of the People Act 1983, 'is indiscriminate. It imposes a blanket restriction on all convicted prisoners in prison... irrespective of the length of their sentence and irrespective of the nature or gravity of their offence and their individual circumstances.'[4]

---

[2] Paragraph 77, *Hirst -v- United Kingdom*, judgment of 6 October 2005, Council of Europe website.

[3] *Ibid*, paragraph 79.

[4] *Ibid*, at paragraph 82.

A substantial minority, comprising Judges Wildhaber, Costa, Lorenzen, Kovler and Jebens, dissented.[5] They found no violation of Article 3 of Protocol 1. The minority convincingly reasoned that Article 3 'does not directly grant individual rights and contains no other conditions for the elections... than the requirement that "the free expression of the opinion of the people" must be ensured'. The minority 'had no difficulty in accepting that the restriction of prisoners' right to vote under the United Kingdom legislation was legitimate for the purposes of preventing crime, punishing offenders and enhancing civic responsibility and respect for the rule of law, as submitted by the respondent Government'. They warned:

> [I]t is essential to bear in mind that the Court is not a legislator and should be careful not to assume legislative functions. An 'evolutive' or 'dynamic' interpretation should have a sufficient basis in changing conditions in the societies of the Contracting States, including an emerging consensus as to the standards to be achieved. We fail to see that this is so in the present case.

As regards the bar on prisoner voting, the minority noted:

> Nor do we find that such a decision needs to be taken by a judge in each individual case. On the contrary, it is obviously compatible with the guarantee of the right to vote to let the legislature decide such issues in the abstract.

The minority concluded:

> Taking into account the sensitive political character of this issue, the diversity of the legal systems within the

---

5   *Ibid*, see in particular paragraphs 2, 3, 6 and 9, dissenting opinion of Judges Wildhaber, Costa, Lorenzen, Kovler and Jebens.

Contracting States and the lack of a sufficiently clear basis for such a right in Article 3 of Protocol No. 1, we are not able to accept that it is for the Court to impose on national legal systems an obligation either to abolish disenfranchisement for prisoners or to allow it only to a very limited extent.

The previous Labour government delayed and refused to implement the judgment or change UK law to comply with it. In the meantime, a number of further relevant judgments were made.

In November 2010, a Chamber of the Strasbourg Court concluded that the UK government 'must introduce legislative proposals to amend [existing legislation] within six months of the date on which the present judgment becomes final, with a view to enactment of an electoral law to achieve compliance with the Court's judgment in *Hirst*'.[6] The Chamber ruled out the award of compensation, subject to UK compliance with the *Hirst* judgment.

In separate proceedings before the Strasbourg Court against Austria in 2010, a Chamber further elaborated the right to vote, articulated in *Hirst*, holding:

> Under the Hirst test, besides ruling out automatic and blanket restrictions it is an essential element that the decision on disenfranchisement should be taken by a judge, taking into account the particular circumstances, and that there must be a link between the offence committed and issues relating to elections and democratic institutions.[7]

---

[6] *Greens and M.T. -v- United Kingdom*, judgment of 23 November 2010, Council of Europe website.

[7] Paragraph 34, *Frodl -v- Austria*, 8 April 2010, Council of Europe website.

The practical effect of the *Frodl* case is to require the decision to bar a convicted prisoner from voting to be made by a judge, and limit judicial sentencing discretion to cases where there is a link between the sanction of denying the vote and the criminal offence committed. The judgment seems to rule out any restrictions on prisoner voting, subject to limited exceptions that appear to relate solely to electoral fraud.

Did Britain sign up to give prisoners the vote?

As the minority pointed out in *Hirst*, Article 3 of Protocol 1 does not contain a right to vote. It contains a 'Right to Free Elections'. Furthermore, during the negotiations on the ECHR, the signatory governments explicitly crafted the language of Article 3 to permit restrictions on who may vote.

On 29 August 1949, the French delegate proposed draft text on the right to free elections, incorporating the words 'universal suffrage'.[8] It was subsequently rejected. One of the principal objections was raised by the British delegate, Sir Oscar Dowson (a former Home Office legal adviser). On 2 February 1950, he stated:

> It is probable that the suffrage is as wide in the United Kingdom as in any other country; yet even in the United Kingdom as in any other country it is inaccurate to speak of the suffrage as 'universal'. In no State is the right to vote enjoyed even by citizens without qualifications. The qualifications required differ from State to State... And it is our view that the variety of circumstances to be considered

---

[8] The negotiating record—or *travaux preparatoires*—to the ECHR are available at:
http://www.echr.coe.int/library/colentravauxprep.html

may justify the imposition of a variety of qualifications, as a condition of the exercise of suffrage.

At that time, Britain barred the vote from peers, felons and the insane. So, the restrictions under consideration were reasonably clear. The British argument was accepted by the negotiating parties. The French proposal was withdrawn in its entirety. When the right to free elections re-appeared in the final text of Protocol 1 two years later, the words 'universal suffrage' had been deleted to take into account the intentions of the negotiating parties.

It is, therefore, clear that Britain did not sign up to giving prisoners a right to vote. In fact, British negotiators successfully precluded such a right from the inclusion in the text of the ECHR. If there were any doubt as to whether or not Article 3 of Protocol 1 gave prisoners a right to vote, the Strasbourg Court would have been entitled under customary international law to consult the negotiating record, or *travaux preparatoires*, to clarify the point.[9] In *Hirst,* the Strasbourg Court ignored the normal rules of treaty interpretation and defied the fundamental democratic principle that states are only bound by the international treaty obligations they freely assume. The majority were not interpreting or applying the ECHR, but rather seeking to expand it—to create a new human right, granting prisoners the vote.

Was Hirst an isolated case of judicial legislation?

The *Hirst* case is one in a long list of examples of the Strasbourg Court engaging in judicial legislation. Britain

---

9   The customary rule of treaty interpretation is now reflected in Article 32 of the Vienna Convention on the Law of Treaties 1969.

was the first country to ratify the Convention in 1951, but opted out of the jurisdiction of the Strasbourg Court for a further 15 years until 1966.

Every government, accepting the jurisdiction of the Strasbourg Court to rule on individual human rights claims, recognised that it would be applied in unforeseen situations. All new law is subject to a degree of risk, because judicial interpretation may lead to unpredictable results. However, the text of the Convention agreed in 1950 represents a fraction of the body of human rights law now in place. The proliferation of new rights by the Strasbourg Court has occurred on a scale unimaginable to the governments negotiating at the time, well beyond the realm of reasonable judicial interpretation.

During the 1970s, a series of cases marked a critical point of departure. In *Golder -v- UK*, the Strasbourg Court read a right of access to the courts into the fair trial guarantees set out in Article 6 of the Convention.[10] This creative innovation drew a stinging rebuke from the British Judge on the court, Sir Gerald Fitzmaurice:

> Finally, it must be said that the above quoted passages from the Judgment of the Court are typical of the cry of the judicial legislator... It may, or it may not be true that a failure to see the Human Rights Convention as comprising a right of access to the courts would have untoward consequences —just as one can imagine such consequences possibly resulting from various other defects or lacunae in this Convention. But this is not the point. The point is that it is for the States upon whose consent the Convention rests, and from which consent alone it derives its obligatory force, to close the gap or put the defect right by an amendment—not

---

[10] *Golder -v- UK*, judgment of 21 February 1975, (1979-80) 1 EHRR 524.

for a judicial tribunal to substitute itself for the convention-makers, to do their work for them.[11]

This case was followed, in 1978, by the exposition of a more general approach. In *Tyrer -v- UK*,[12] the Strasbourg Court held that judicial corporal punishment on the Isle of Man was sufficiently degrading that it breached the prohibition on torture and inhuman treatment. Irrespective of the merits of the case, the judicial conclusion was reached without any basis in the text of the Convention or the negotiating records. The judges reasoned in legalistic language, but the case marked a fundamental change in approach—from disciplined judicial interpretation, to an overtly political renovation and re-writing of human rights law:

> The Court must also recall that the Convention is a living instrument which, as the Commission rightly stressed, must be interpreted in the light of present-day conditions. In the case now before it the Court cannot but be influenced by the developments and commonly accepted standards in the penal policy of the member States of the Council of Europe in this field.[13]

The judgment marked a watershed. The Convention was now to be regarded as a 'living instrument', evolving, growing and expanding into new territory at the behest of the Strasbourg Court. In another case, the Strasbourg Court suggested that:

> To the extent that the number of member States [party to the Convention] increases... in such a larger, diversified

---

[11] *Ibid*, at paragraph 37. Separate Opinion, Judge Fitzmaurice.

[12] *Tyrer -v- UK*, Judgment of 25 April 1978, (1979-1980) 2 EHRR 1.

[13] *Ibid*, paragraph 31.

community the development of common standards may well prove the best, if not the only way of achieving the Court's professed aim of ensuring that the Convention remains a living instrument to be interpreted so as to reflect societal changes and to remain in line with present-day conditions.[14]

The ominous phrase, 'living instrument', was deployed to justify the idea that the proper role of the Strasbourg Court was to legislate to update Convention rights. Unsurprisingly, given the negotiating history, the Convention does not mention any judicial power to create new law. On the contrary, the very first article of the Convention makes it crystal clear that the Court should apply the list of rights as '*defined* in Section I of this Convention' (emphasis added), rather than adding to their meaning. Article 32 of the ECHR further defines the Strasbourg Court's judicial mandate as extending 'to all matters concerning the interpretation and application of the Convention and the Protocols', but makes no mention of expanding or adding to the rights provided by the ECHR.

The judges have assumed a legislative function, fully aware that there are limited means for elected governments subject to their rulings to exercise any meaningful democratic oversight over them. This judicial coup represents a naked usurpation, by a judicial body, of the legislative power that properly belongs to democratically-elected law makers. As one Strasbourg judge has recognised:

---

14   *Cossey -v- UK* (27 September 1990) 13 EHRR 622, at paragraph 3.6.3 of the Court's judgment.

I also concede that the Convention organs have in this way, on occasion, reached the limits of what can be regarded as treaty interpretation in the legal sense. At times they have perhaps even crossed the boundary and entered territory which is no longer that of treaty interpretation but is actually legal policy-making. But this, as I understand it, is not for a court to do; on the contrary, policy-making is a task for the legislature or the Contracting States themselves, as the case may be.[15]

The list of novel human rights created—or expanded— in this way is long. The Strasbourg Court has dictated the rules on parental discipline of children in the home, notionally based on the prohibition of torture and inhuman and degrading treatment contained in Article 3 of the ECHR. Article 3 was designed to ban the horrors of the Nazi era—not tell parents how to look after their children.[16]

Likewise, when the negotiators drafted the ECHR, the signatories intended to guarantee a core list of rights to 'everyone within their jurisdiction'. They aimed to include non-citizens and even non-residents living in their country. But, it is clear from the negotiating record that they only agreed to give effect to the Convention within their own territories.[17] Yet, the Strasbourg Court—

---

[15] Judge Franz Matscher, 'Methods of Interpretation of the Convention', in MacDonald, Matscher and Petzold, *The European System for the Protection of Human Rights*, 1993.

[16] *A -v- UK*, judgment of 23 September 1998, (1999) 27 EHRR 611.

[17] See the *travaux preparatoires* to Article 1 of the ECHR, particularly at page 49, available at www.echr.coe.int. The expanded definition of jurisdiction was explained by the Strasbourg Court in *Issa v Turkey* (2004) 41 EHRR 567.

now closely followed by the UK courts—has effectively ~~re-written this part of the Convention~~, to allow human rights claims against a state where it exercises 'authority and/or effective control' abroad.[18]

Article 2 of the ECHR protects the right to life. The intention, again influenced by the experience of Nazi crimes during the war, was to ban extra-judicial executions and similar killings, committed or sanctioned by the hand of the state. The Strasbourg Court has expanded this right well beyond the original Convention. The state can now be blamed—and sued—even when it has had no direct responsibility for someone's death. There is now a human right to police protection from violence and threats in our society. In *Osman -v- UK*, a mentally-ill teacher became obsessed with one of his pupils. He shot the boy, injuring him, and killed his father. The family claimed that the police had violated the father's right to life by failing to prevent his death. The claim of police negligence failed in the UK courts. The claim was then taken to the Strasbourg Court in 1998. The family's claim was rejected on the facts of the case, but the court nonetheless held that the right to life placed a general duty on the police to do everything 'that can be reasonably expected of them to avoid a real and immediate risk to life of which they have or ought to have knowledge'.[19] It ruled that limits on negligence claims against the police under UK law were unduly restrictive

---

[18] Paragraph 71, judgment of the Strasbourg Court in *Issa v Turkey* (2004) 41 EHRR 567.

[19] Paraagraph 116, *Osman -v- UK* (1998) 29 EHRR 245.

and amounted to a violation of the claimants' right to access to court.[20]

Whilst policy pledges designed to increase police responsiveness to threats of violence can serve the public interest, cementing them as constitutionally-enforceable human rights places an extraordinary additional burden on our police and leads to unintended consequences. Human rights are universal, so the police must offer the same level of police protection to innocent members of the public as to the worst criminals. As a result of *Osman*, an increasing amount of police time is diverted to provide witness protection to gangsters giving evidence in mafia trials—in effect protecting gangsters from the risks they pose to each other. In a world of finite resources, this inevitably displaces the police capacity allocated to protect law-abiding members of society. It has been estimated that the British police now spend £20 million a year protecting gangsters from each other, a direct consequence of the extension of the right to life under Article 2.[21] As a result of the growing pressure on finite resources, police have proved unable to protect juries in criminal trials. In 2010, Britain witnessed the first criminal trial in 400 years to dispense with a jury—an ancient legal right dating back to Magna Carta.[22] The expansion of human rights by Strasbourg has led to the erosion of

---

[20] See also *Z-v-UK* (2001) 34 EHRR 97, in which the Strasbourg Court adapted its approach in *Osman*.

[21] Reported in the *Daily Telegraph*, 14 January 2008.

[22] Reported in *The Times*, 13 January 2010, at: http://business.timesonline.co.uk/tol/business/law/article698 4904.ece.

traditional British rights—effectively robbing Peter to pay Paul.

The *Osman* ruling drew strong criticism from senior UK judges. Lord Hoffman characterised the ruling as 'essentially... about the obligations of the welfare state', warning: 'I am bound to say that this decision fills me with apprehension', because it involves the Strasbourg Court 'challenging the autonomy of the courts and indeed the Parliament of the United Kingdom to deal with what are essentially social welfare questions involving budgetary limits and efficient public administration'.[23] He added that the case 'serves to reinforce the doubts I have had for a long time about the suitability, at least for this country, of having questions of human rights determined by an international tribunal made up of judges from many countries', surmising:

> I accept that there is an irreducible minimum of human rights which must be universally true. But most of the jurisprudence which comes out of Strasbourg is not about the irreducible minimum... It is often said that the tendency of every court is to increase its jurisdiction and the Strasbourg court is no exception. So far as the margin of appreciation accommodates national choices, the jurisdiction of the European court is unnecessary; so far as it does not, it is undesirable.

Lord Hoffman concluded:

> ...the jurisprudence of the Strasbourg court does create a dilemma because it seems to me to have passed far beyond its original modest ambitions and is seeking to impose a Voltairean uniformity of values upon all member States. This I hope we shall resist.

---

23 Pages 163 to 166, 'Human Rights and the House of Lords', Lord Hoffman, *62 Modern Law Review,* March 1999.

In practice, the courts in this country have not resisted the Strasbourg case-law, but sought to match it—and sometimes extend it—under UK law. Relying on the *Osman* ruling, the Strasbourg Court—followed by UK judges acting under the Human Rights Act—have deployed the right to life to side-step the carefully calibrated rules on police liability, overruling the UK law of negligence.[24] By allowing these claims against the police to succeed on human rights grounds, the courts have prevented Britain's democratically-elected law-makers from determining the proper balance in this delicate—and inherently political—area of public policy.

Judicial legislation has not been limited to Articles 1 and 2 of the ECHR. According to a leading human rights text book, the definition of torture and inhuman treatment in Article 3 is now so broad that it can include 'grossly defamatory remarks and extreme and continuous police surveillance'.[25] It has also been expanded to allow human rights claims for accommodation and health care in circumstances where, if the state did not provide it, the claimant would be homeless and without any other means of support.[26] For example, a drugs-trafficker with

---

[24] See *'Osman -v- UK*—Transforming English Negligence Law into French Administrative Law?', G. Monti, October 1999, 48 ICLQ 757.

[25] Page 403, *European Human Rights Law*, Keir Starmer QC, published by Legal Action Group 1999. See, in particular, *East African Asian* Case (1981) 3 EHRR 76; and *D'Haeses, Le Compte -v- Belgium* (1984) 6 EHRR 114.

[26] For example, see the House of Lords' reasoning in *R (Adam, Limbuela and Tesema) -v- Home Secretary*, 3 November 2005, [2005] UKHL 66.

AIDS deployed Article 3 to block his deportation and force the government to let him remain in the UK in order to receive medical treatment on the NHS.[27]

The Strasbourg Court has further legislated to extend the ban on torture and inhuman treatment, making it much more difficult for governments to deport people who pose a threat to national security or public safety. This goes well beyond the list of rights set out in either the United Nations Refugee Convention or the United Nations Convention against Torture, both of which were specifically designed to address the difficult and delicate issue of deporting individuals who might be mistreated if returned home.

In *Chahal -v- UK* (1996), the government sought to deport Mr Chahal, a Sikh separatist, to India, on the basis of his conduct in the UK which gave rise to a suspicion of involvement in terrorism and other criminal conduct.[28] Mr Chahal had previously been arrested, but not charged, with conspiracy to assassinate the Indian Prime Minister on a visit to Britain. The Strasbourg Court barred Mr Chahal's deportation, concluding he would face a real risk of torture at the hands of rogue elements in the Punjab police.

However, deportation is not merely blocked when there is a specific risk of torture or inhuman treatment by the state or its officials on return. In another Strasbourg

---

[27] *D -v- UK* (1997) 24 EHRR 423. See *N -v- UK*, judgment of 27 May 2008, particularly at paragraph 45, regarding the general principles to be applied to the deportation of those with serious illness.

[28] *Chahal -v- UK*, Judgment of 15 November 1996, (1997) 23 EHRR 413.

case, a convicted armed robber managed to prevent his deportation to Somalia because of the risk that he would be caught up in the civil war there, rather than any fear of persecution by the government.[29] In another UK case, a woman was able to block her return to Uganda because the risk that she would not be able to find decent housing or employment rendered her vulnerable to being drawn into a life of prostitution.[30]

Recent developments are cause for further concern. In a string of new cases, Article 8—containing the right to family life—has been stretched to defeat deportation proceedings. In October 2008, the House of Lords allowed a novel claim under Article 8 to quash a deportation order, based on the risk that a mother might be separated from her son in custodial proceedings under Shari'a law, if returned to Lebanon.[31] In a subsequent House of Lords case in February 2009, the House of Lords recognised that UK courts were extending human rights law to defeat deportation orders beyond what has been required by the Strasbourg case-law. Lord Hope stated that he could find no Strasbourg case where deportation had been overruled on human rights grounds other than under Articles 2 or 3.[32] Yet, he acknowledged that the House of Lords had

---

[29] *Ahmed -v- Austria,* Judgment of 17 December 1996, (1997) 24 EHRR 278.

[30] *AA(Uganda) -v- Secretary of State for the Home Department,* 22 May, [2008] WLR(D) 170.

[31] *EM (Lebanon) (FC) -v- Home Secretary,* House of Lords, 22 October 2008, [2008] UKHL 64.

[32] Paragraph 8, *RB (Algeria) (FC) -v- Home Secretary,* House of Lords, 18 February 2009, [2009] UKHL 10.

extended Article 8 to defeat deportation proceedings and accepted, in principle, that the risk of violations to Article 5 (right to liberty) or Article 6 (right to fair trial) could justify quashing deportation orders. The reasoning of the Law Lords appears at least in part based on an attempt to predict and pre-empt the extension of the Strasbourg case-law, rather than constrain it.

Having been given a green light by the UK courts operating under the Human Rights Act, in 2009 and 2010 the Strasbourg Court subsequently followed British precedent, by allowing a convicted heroin dealer and a sex offender to rely on Article 8 to quash their deportation orders.[33]

Following these rulings, the UK courts have gone even further. In May 2010, in the *Gurung* case, the Immigration Tribunal held that a homicide offence is not serious enough to warrant automatic deportation under the UK Borders Act 2007. A gang chased and killed a young Nepalese man in London, dumping his body in the river Thames. In a novel ruling, one of the culprits successfully claimed the right to family life to trump deportation back to Nepal, despite being an adult with no dependents.[34]

It is one thing to block deportation to prevent returning an individual into the arms of a torturing state. It is another moral leap to frustrate deportation proceedings against convicted criminals or suspected terrorists because it might disrupt their family ties.

---

[33] *AW Khan -v- UK*, 12 January 2010; *Omojudi -v- UK*, 24 November 2009; both available from the Council of Europe website.

[34] See the case of Rocky Gurung, reported in the *Sunday Telegraph*, 16 January 2011.

Quantitatively as well as qualitatively, the Article 8 cases mark a fork in the road. According to the UK Border Agency, hundreds of foreign national prisoners are defeating deportation orders each year, on human rights grounds, and the majority of the claims are now based on Article 8.[35]

The expansion of human rights to frustrate deportation proceedings has had unintended consequences. Control Orders were introduced in Britain, following the *Belmarsh* judgment in 2004, in large part because of the increasing fetters on Britain's ability to deport terrorist suspects. As a result of judicial legislation, Britain has lost a degree of control over its borders, which inevitably means we are importing more risk. Although difficult to quantify, this has contributed to the growing terrorist threat and pressure on MI5 and counter-terrorism police. The last government responded to these pressures with a series of draconian measures, from Control Orders to proposals to increase detention without charge. Ironically, the expansion of human rights to defeat deportation proceedings has imposed additional pressures on traditional British liberties, including the ancient right of habeas corpus.

Liberal Democrat peer Lord Carlile has criticised this aspect of the impact of current human rights law on deportation in his role as statutory reviewer of counter-terrorism:

> The effect is to make the UK a safe haven for some individuals whose determination is to damage the UK and its citizens, hardly a satisfactory situation save for the purist.[36]

---

[35] Freedom of Information response, 23 February 2011.

[36] Sixth Report, 3 February 2011.

Beyond deportation, convicted criminals have benefited more than most from the growth industry in human rights. Prisoners have successfully claimed access to fertility treatment (whilst still in prison) and—in one of the most bizarre policies articulated by any government department—the right to keep twigs, to wave as wands, in order to exercise the right to practise paganism in their prison cells.[37]

Perhaps the most graphic illustration of the practical effect of the expansion of human rights is the Naomi Bryant case. On 17 August 2005, Ms Bryant was strangled and stabbed to death by Anthony Rice, a serial criminal with a long list of prior convictions for violent and sexual offences. In 1989, Rice had been given a discretionary life sentence of imprisonment for attempted rape, indecent assault and assault occasioning actual bodily harm. Rice had attacked a woman in the street at midnight and subjected her to a horrific ordeal. The trial judge sentenced him to a minimum of ten years in prison, after which his release would be determined by the Parole Board. He was subsequently released on license and went on to kill Naomi Bryant, despite warning signs that should have been picked up by the authorities monitoring him.

An independent review, conducted by Her Majesty's Inspectorate of Probation (HMIP), highlighted a range of mistakes and administrative failings. However, the report also focused on the way in which human rights considerations had undermined the decision-making by

---

[37] See *Dickson -v- UK*, Strasbourg Court, 4 December 2007; and Maria Eagle's answer to a written Parliamentary question by Andrew Turner, 1 May 2008.

the Parole Board and probation authorities. One of HMIP's key recommendations was that:

> ...although proper attention should be given to the human rights issues, the relevant authorities involved should maintain in practice a top priority focus on the public protection requirements of the case.[38]

According to HMIP, Rice's right to a private life and freedom of association had obscured the focus on public protection. The assessments that led to the decision to release and the formulation of the conditions of Rice's license became dominated by the debate on whether or not the restrictions on his private life under Article 8 ECHR were 'necessary and proportionate' as required under the Human Rights Act. The consideration of the enforcement of the conditions was flawed. Representations were made by Rice's lawyer and the Home Office that the conditions of his licence were too restrictive, specifically bearing in mind recent court rulings under the Human Rights Act and the imminent possibility of judicial review of any decision they made. HMIP stated:

> We find it regrettable that attention to effectiveness and enforceability was undermined by the attention devoted to issues of lawfulness and proportionality.[39]

The effect was to dilute the license conditions, allowing Rice to manipulate restrictions designed to protect the public. HMIP concluded:

> It is a challenging task for people who are charged with managing offenders effectively to ensure that public

---

[38] Key Recommendation 4, *HMIP Independent Review into the Case of Anthony Rice*, May 2006.

[39] *Ibid*, at paragraph 8.3.12.

protection considerations are not undermined by the human rights considerations.[40]

More recently, Britain submitted an appeal against a decision by the Chamber of the Strasbourg Court which struck down UK rules on the admissibility of 'hearsay' evidence — deemed fair by the Supreme Court — in two cases concerning convicted sex and violent offenders.[41] If the UK appeal fails, the Lord Chief Justice, Lord Judge, has warned the ruling would have 'huge implications for the way in which the entire criminal justice system in this country works', while another Law Lord, Lord Brown, worries that 'many defendants will have to go free'.[42]

The scale of judicial legislation and the willingness of the Strasbourg Court to override both the UK courts and Parliament have generated widespread concern amongst senior members of the UK judiciary. Lord Hoffman has been outspoken in his criticism that the Strasbourg Court has proved:

> unable to resist the temptation to aggrandise its jurisdiction and to impose uniform rules on Member States... laying down a federal law of Europe.[43]

The current President of the Supreme Court, Lord Phillips, has delivered a similar message in more guarded terms. In one domestic case, Lord Phillips made clear:

---

[40] *Ibid*, at paragraph 10.2.17.

[41] *The Times*, 22 February 2011.

[42] *Ibid*.

[43] Lord Hoffman, 2009 Judicial Studies Board Annual Lecture. See also his foreword to the Policy Exchange report *Bringing Rights Back Home* by Dr Michael Pinto-Duschinsky, 7 February 2011.

There will, however, be rare occasions where this court has concerns as to whether a decision of the Strasbourg Court sufficiently appreciates or accommodates particular aspects of our domestic process. In such circumstances it is open to this court to decline to follow the Strasbourg decision, giving reasons for adopting this course. This is likely to give the Strasbourg Court the opportunity to reconsider the particular aspect of the decision that is in issue, so that there takes place what may prove to be a valuable dialogue between this court and the Strasbourg Court.[44]

More recently, Lord Phillips added:

Whenever Strasbourg gives a judgment which, when we have to consider its impact, leads us to believe that perhaps they haven't fully appreciated how things work in this country, we invite them to think again.[45]

Lord Hope put it more bluntly still:

We certainly won't lie down in front of what they tell us.[46]

Further criticism has come from the Lord Chief Justice, Lord Judge, who has expressed concern that the importation of the Strasbourg case-law is diluting the distinctive character of British common law:

The statutory obligation on our courts is to take account of the decisions of the court in Strasbourg... We can follow the reasoning and if possible identify and apply the principle... not because we are bound to do so, even if the decision is

---

[44] Paragraph 11, *R -v- Horncastle* (2009) UKSC 14, http://www.supremecourt.gov.uk/docs/uksc_2009_0073_judgment.pdf

[45] Originally made on 29 July 2010. Reported in the *Sunday Times*, 13 February 2011.

[46] *Ibid.*

that of the Grand Chamber, or because the Supreme Court is a court subordinate to the Strasbourg court, but because, having taken the Strasbourg decision into account and examined it, it will often follow that it is appropriate to do so. But it will not always be appropriate to do so. What I respectfully suggest is that statute ensures that the final word does not rest with Strasbourg, but with our Supreme Court.[47]

He added:

Are we becoming so focused on Strasbourg and the Convention that instead of incorporating Convention principles within and developing the common law accordingly as a single coherent unit, we are allowing the Convention to assume an unspoken priority over the common law? Or is it that we are just still on honeymoon with the Convention? We must beware. It would be a sad day if the home of the common law lost its standing as a common law authority.

If senior UK judges are concerned that the Strasbourg Court is micro-managing their domestic *interpretation* of human rights law, undermining the status of the newly-founded Supreme Court, it is hardly surprising that Members of Parliament are disturbed that Strasbourg is usurping their (non-judicial) legislative function, by *creating and expanding* new rights, immune from any democratic accountability.[48] In a backbench-sponsored debate, on 10 February, MPs voted by 10 to 1, with a majority of over 200, to retain the existing ban on prisoner voting despite the Strasbourg Court's ruling in *Hirst*.

---

[47] Speech to the Judicial Studies Board, 17 March 2010.

[48] See the Hansard record for the Westminster Hall debate, 11 January 2011, and the main Chamber debate, 10 February 2011.

The *Hirst* ruling presents the government with a dilemma. It has an international obligation to implement adverse rulings of the Strasbourg Court, as a state party to the ECHR. Yet, the Strasbourg Court has acted beyond any reasonable interpretation of its judicial mandate, systematically assuming a legislative function, provoking a constitutional clash with elected law-makers in the House of Commons which gives rise to an ostensible conflict between the requirements of international law and British democracy. How should the government respond?

The Case for Democracy

What are the options for addressing the Hirst ruling ?

The government has mooted a number of proposals for addressing the *Hirst* ruling, including proposals to give the vote to prisoners serving less than four years, and an alternative proposal to limit the right to vote to prisoners serving 12 months or less.[49] However, the *Frodl* ruling suggests that any attempt to define eligibility to vote amongst prisoners by reference to the gravity of the crime or length of sentence would not satisfy the Strasbourg Court.

The House of Commons Political and Constitutional Reform Committee has suggested that 'an element of individual assessment would need to be introduced into the process of deciding whether and for how long a convicted criminal should be disenfranchised'.[50] The Committee considered vesting such discretion with the sentencing judge. However, a sentencing judge in the UK would need statutory criteria or further guidance in order to exercise any such discretion, returning the issue to the

---

[49] Cabinet Office Minister Mark Harper announced the four year proposal on 20 December 2010, by written ministerial statement. Cabinet Office references to the alternative 12 month proposal were reported in the *Daily Telegraph* on 20 January 2011.

[50] Paragraph 12, report on 'Voting by Convicted Prisoners', published on 4 February 2011.

government and Parliament. Furthermore, since the purpose of excluding prisoners from voting in the UK is related to the seriousness of the crime—in that it attracts a custodial sentence—there seems little point in requiring judicial consideration of the particular circumstances of the individual offence itself. Delegating the issue to be determined by judicial discretion cannot, therefore, resolve the issue.

In reality, the shifting goalposts of the Strasbourg case-law—from *Hirst* to *Frodl*—suggest that the underlying direction and intention of the Strasbourg Court is to enfranchise all prisoners over time, as a matter of judicial policy. This was also the implication of the dissenting minority in *Hirst,* which criticised the 'dynamic and evolutive' approach of the majority.

In light of these considerations, the fundamental tension—and binary choice—lies between the drive of the Strasbourg Court towards total enfranchisement of prisoners and the decision of the House of Commons to retain the status quo in the UK. Any other compromise proposal is likely to be struck down by the Strasbourg Court at some point in the future.

Since the House of Commons has expressed its overwhelming view that the existing ban should remain, what would be the consequences of failing to fully implement the *Hirst* ruling? In practice, the UK has already satisfied one of the elements of the ruling, by ensuring the issue is subjected to proper Parliamentary debate, so that competing arguments can be considered.

In addition, there are no principled or practical objections to heeding a second element of the judgment, by legislating to ensure that prisoners are formally notified of the forfeiture of the right to vote at the time of sentencing. In meeting two of the concerns of the Strasbourg Court, Parliament would be placing the government in a stronger position to revert to the Strasbourg Court to explain that Parliament has overwhelmingly rejected proposals to give prisoners the vote.

Nevertheless, it remains unlikely that the Strasbourg Court would reverse its decisions in *Hirst, Frodl* and *Greens* in relation to the validity of retaining a ban on all prisoners from voting, at least in the short-term.

Does ignoring Strasbourg undermine the rule of law?

Britain faces a constitutional conundrum. On the one hand, the principle of democratic accountability for law-making—required by the separation of powers—is being systematically eroded by judicial legislation from Strasbourg. Yet, re-asserting Britain's democratic prerogatives runs in tension with the duty to abide by final judgments of the Strasbourg Court under Article 46 of the ECHR.

There is a compelling argument that the Strasbourg Court is acting *ultra vires*—beyond its powers—in light of the express limits on its mandate to interpret and apply, but not revise, the Convention under Article 32. The Court has the power to decide whether it has jurisdiction to hear a case, but the architects of the ECHR built in a safeguard against wider abuse of judicial power. The Strasbourg Court has no mechanism to enforce its own rulings directly.

In the event of non-compliance with a Strasbourg judgment, the Committee of Ministers of the Council of Europe will review the case and seek information from the relevant state party. There are 47 members of the

Committee of Ministers. While the Chairman of the Committee may engage in correspondence with a state party concerning adverse rulings and the Committee may pass resolutions, there is no power to directly enforce any judgments, fine a state party, enforce compensation or otherwise compel compliance. While there is a power to suspend or expel state parties from the Council of Europe, such a power has never been used—despite egregious human rights abuses in certain countries, such as Turkey and Russia.

In particular, there is no power directly to enforce compensation awards made by the Strasbourg Court, either directly or through the UK courts. That position was confirmed by both the High Court and Ministry of Justice legal advice in February 2011.[51]

Furthermore, there is no practical risk that Britain would be suspended from the Council of Europe for failure to adhere to the *Hirst* ruling. As of 2009, there were 8,661 cases 'pending' before the Committee of Ministers— i.e. unimplemented judgments.[52] Eighty-eight per cent of the total number of unimplemented rulings affect the following state parties, in order of non-compliance: Italy, Turkey, Russia, Poland, Ukraine, Romania, Greece, Bulgaria, Slovenia and Hungary. Britain has 27 cases pending, less than one per cent of the total and three more

---

51 *Tovey, Hydes and others -v- Ministry of Justice*, 18 February 2011, [2011] EWHC 271 (QB); Ministry of Justice legal advice was leaked to *The Times*, and made available online, 17 February 2011.

52 Council of Europe website at: http://www.coe.int/t/dghl/monitoring/execution/Reports/Stats/Statistiques_2009_EN.pdf

than Germany. In reality, given the volume and seriousness of outstanding cases against other countries, the British ban on prisoner voting is unlikely to create any substantial diplomatic problems for the UK in the Committee of Ministers. There are too many other egregious violations of basic ECHR rights by a wide range of state parties outstanding.

One of the principal arguments presented against refusing to implement the *Hirst* ruling is moral. Shami Chakrabati, Director of Liberty, argues that by failing to implement Strasbourg decisions:

> [Y]ou give up any moral authority to influence Russia and Turkey, let alone China and the Middle East, on human rights in the future.[53]

Ms Chakrabati further defends the Human Rights Act by pointing out that it preserves democratic account-ability, because the government and Parliament are 'completely free to ignore' declarations of incompatibility made by our domestic courts, where they find UK legislation in violation of the ECHR under the Act. However, this begs the question: why, as a matter of principle, is it legitimate for elected law-makers in the House of Commons to have the last word on contentious human rights interpretations made by UK courts, but not the flagrant judicial legislation coming from the Strasbourg Court?

The suggestion that Britain will be less able to press more authoritarian foreign governments to improve their human rights records is questionable. Russia and China violate the human rights of their own people because they can do so without consequence, not by reference to the

---

53 *The Times*, 21 February 2011.

example set by other nations. It is equally difficult to accept that Britain will somehow lose her moral right or diplomatic ability to object to despots gunning down unarmed civilians, or electrocuting detainees under interrogation, unless we give convicted prisoners the vote. It has not made any difference over the last six years—let alone the 50 years before the *Hirst* judgment— and the respective bans on prisoner voting do not appear to have affected the diplomatic clout of other countries that ban prisoner voting including Liechtenstein, Estonia, the United States, Japan, Brazil and Australia.[54]

In sum, there are compelling grounds for upholding the overwhelming vote of the UK's elected law-makers in the face of a serious abuse of judicial power by the Strasbourg Court. The government has acknowledged this. On 1 March 2011, Cabinet Office Minister Mark Harper told Parliament:

> The Government have requested that the court's judgment in the 'Greens and MT' case be referred to the Grand Chamber of the European Court of Human Rights (ECtHR)—the highest tier of the ECtHR. If the Grand Chamber agrees to the referral, they will look again at the judgment and issue their opinion. The basis of the Government's referral request is that we believe that the court should look again at the principles in 'Hirst' which outlaw a blanket ban on prisoners voting, particularly given the recent debate in the House of Commons.[55]

The government should strengthen its appeal by preparing legislative proposals to ensure that convicted offenders receiving a custodial sentence are informed of

---

54 Australia has a total ban in a majority of states.

55 Hansard, 1 March 2011.

the temporary loss of the right to vote at the sentencing stage. The United Kingdom would then have addressed two out of the three criticisms in *Hirst*.

In seeking a reversal of the *Hirst* ruling, the government must make it clear that it *cannot*—rather than will not—enact legislation to give prisoners the vote, in light of the contrary express will of Parliament. There is a range of precedent for such an approach. The French and German constitutional courts have made it clear that Strasbourg rulings cannot override the constitution or basic laws in their respective countries. In a recent referendum, the Swiss voted to enact legislation compelling automatic deportation of serious criminals, which will inevitably clash with the ECHR and Strasbourg case-law.[56] Yet, under their constitution, Swiss referenda take priority.

Whilst the Grand Chamber is unlikely to reverse its ruling in *Hirst*, in the short-term, it will face a growing predicament of its own. The Strasbourg Court will be forced either to challenge the legitimacy of the Parliamentary vote or seek to overrule the express will of Britain's democratically elected representatives. If the Strasbourg Court requires the government to 'whip'—or force—a vote through Parliament, it would risk a serious constitutional crisis.

Government and Parliament should resist any such attempt to undermine the will of the UK's elected lawmakers. The worst case scenario is that *Greens* and *Hirst* may be upheld, and the cases remain on the list of pending cases subject to review by the Committee of Ministers. However, there is no prospect of any formal

---

[56] Reported in the *Financial Times*, 29 November 2010.

sanction. Even if the Strasbourg Court rejects the latest appeal in *Greens*, Britain will have sent a clear message to the Strasbourg judiciary that its erosion of the separation of powers and UK democratic accountability will no longer be accepted. That is important in the context of *Hirst*, but also future cases. The Attorney General has anticipated 'a rather drawn-out dialogue between ourselves and the [Strasbourg] Court'.[57] Given the lack of enforceability of Strasbourg judgments, this cannot harm the UK's interests, but will allow the time and space within which the UK can seek wider reform of the application of the ECHR under its own domestic law and at the international level.

---

[57] Hansard, 10 February 2011.

Democratic Accountability at Home

Chapter 3 of the Coalition programme for government states:

> We will establish a Commission to investigate the creation of a British Bill of Rights that incorporates and builds on all our obligations under the European Convention on Human Rights, ensures that these rights continue to be enshrined in British law, and protects and extends British liberties.[58]

On 18 March 2011, the Cabinet Office Minister Mark Harper issued a written statement to the House of Commons, announcing the establishment of a Commission:

> [T]o investigate the creation of a UK Bill of Rights that incorporates and builds on all our obligations under the European Convention on Human Rights, ensures that these rights continue to be enshrined in UK law, and protects and extend our liberties. It will examine the operation and implementation of these obligations, and consider ways to promote a better understanding of the true scope of these obligations and liberties.

The establishment of a commission to consider a Bill of Rights is welcome, although the terms of reference are narrow and make no mention of the problem of judicial legislation or the margin of appreciation.

---

[58] Available on the Cabinet Office website.

Furthermore, a Bill of Rights would mark a substantial constitutional innovation, and it will prove a challenge to forge a consensus on a cross-party basis, between the Conservatives and Liberal Democrats, let alone Labour. As one Conservative Minister said: 'There is no guarantee the commission will find a way forward and the two parties may have to agree to disagree.' Another Liberal Democrat Minister agreed: 'We may end up going our own ways.'[59] In any event, it will take a considerable amount of time for the Commission to produce proposals for legislation. A successful outcome is not assured within the current Coalition during the course of this Parliament.

In the meantime, therefore, the Coalition should in tandem seek a less ambitious interim solution through a series of bespoke amendments to the Human Rights Act, designed to strengthen democratic accountability and address the specific and growing problem of legal challenges to deportation under Article 8.[60]

- **Enshrine free votes on Strasbourg rulings**

As Shami Chakrabati of Liberty points out, where domestic courts make a declaration of incompatibility, the government and Parliament 'are completely free to ignore' it under Sections 4 and 10 of the Human Rights Act. A corresponding additional clause should be inserted into the Human Rights Act to provide for a Parliamentary debate and vote on adverse judgments against the UK made by the Strasbourg Court, to ensure that elected representatives

---

[59] Reported, *The Independent*, 9 March 2011.

[60] Sir Malcolm Rifkind QC MP called for amendment of the Human Rights Act in his Denning Lecture, 28 October 2009, at Lincoln's Inn.

~~have the last word on Strasbourg as well as domestic~~
human rights rulings. In addition, the main political parties
should follow the precedent of the backbench debate on 10
February 2011 and make a political commitment to free
votes on such contentious debates.

In addition to institutionalising the Parliamentary
practice followed on prisoner voting, this change would
place a democratic check on the growing judicial
legislation expanding Article 8, particularly as it impacts
on Britain's ability to deport criminals and terrorist
suspects.

• Strengthen the independence of the Supreme Court

Section 2 of the Human Rights Act provides that UK
courts must 'take into account' the decisions of the
Strasbourg Court, even where they do not relate to the
UK. This deference to the wider case-law of the Strasbourg Court is not required by the UK's international
obligations under the Convention itself. Britain's
obligation is limited to following the rulings in cases to
which it is a party.

In addition, the duty to take the wider Strasbourg case-
law into account has been strengthened by the UK courts
into a duty to match it. As Lord Bingham summarised:

> The duty of national courts is to keep pace with the
> Strasbourg jurisprudence as it evolves over time: no more,
> but certainly no less.[61]

There has been some divergence from this principle
under the new Supreme Court, as it attempts to re-assert

---

[61] Paragraph 20, *R (Ullah)-v- Special Adjudicator,* 17 June 2004,
[2004] 2 AC 323, at 350.

its autonomy.[62] Section 2 of the Human Rights Act should be amended to make clear that the UK courts have a duty to consider—but not apply—the Strasbourg case-law relating to other state parties, and expand that duty to include taking into account other common law treatment of similar human rights issues. That would ensure that the UK courts take a more balanced approach, taking into account the approach to difficult human rights cases taken by the courts in other common law countries, not just uncritically following guidance from the Strasbourg Court. In addition, the amendment should make explicit that the Supreme Court retains complete discretion to apply the relevant ECHR right to the circumstances prevailing in the UK. This would help to prevent the wholesale importation of the Strasbourg case-law with its continental and civil law bias—and judicial legislation— whilst preserving the common law tradition and guaranteeing the Supreme Court retains its independence and authority as the final court of appeal in the UK.

- **Defend the will of Parliament**

Under Section 3 of the Human Rights Act, the UK courts are mandated to 'read down' legislation enacted by Parliament in order to comply with expanded human rights interpretations. Legislation 'must be read and given effect in a way which is compatible with the Convention rights'. In practice, this requires the courts to bend legislation to pre-emptively avoid clashes with human rights rulings, unless the primary legislation in question makes such judicial creativity impossible.

---

[62] See Lord Phillips in *R- v- Horncastle* (2009) UKSC 14, cited above.

Section 3 effectively compels judges to re-write the law, changing its original meaning and undermining the intentions of Parliament. As one former Parliamentary Counsel described the practical effect, the Human Rights Act 'instructs the courts to falsify the linguistic meaning of other Acts of Parliament, which hitherto has depended on legislative intention at the time of enactment'.[63] Section 3 should be amended to make clear that such forced judicial interpretation is not permissible where it would undermine the 'object and purpose' of the legislation according to the will of Parliament at the time of enactment. If the laws passed by Parliament are deemed in conflict with the ECHR, the correct approach is for the courts to make a declaration of incompatibility and return the discrepancy to the government and ultimately Parliament to resolve.

For the same reasons, Section 6 of the Human Rights Act should be amended to prevent the courts striking down the decisions of public bodies in circumstances where it would serve to undermine the 'object and purpose' of the authorising legislation according to the will of Parliament at the time of enactment.

- **Remove fetters on deportation**

As considered in detail above, one of the principal problems arising from growing judicial legislation has been the increasing fetters imposed on Britain's ability to deport convicted criminals and terrorist suspects. On 25 July 2007, shortly after becoming Prime Minister, Gordon Brown gave an interview in the *Sun*, stating:

---

[63] Francis Bennion, 'Human Rights: A Threat to Law?', 2003, 26(2) UNSWLJ 418 at 433.

If you commit a crime you will be deported. You play by the rules or you face the consequences... I'm not prepared to tolerate a situation where we have people breaking the rules in our country when we cannot act.

The UK Borders Act 2007 was consequently enacted on 30 October 2007 and made provision for automatic deportation of criminals under Sections 32 to 39. However, Section 33 expressly created a statutory exception where deportation might breach an individual's rights under the ECHR. There was no need to include this exception in the 2007 Act, because the Human Rights Act applies anyway. In doing so, it allowed the courts to 'read down' the legislation rather than making a declaration of incompatibility which would return the discrepancy to the government and Parliament to resolve. Gordon Brown thereby allowed the emasculation of the legislation which would break his pledge to deport foreign criminals. This is also how the convicted homicide offender in the *Gurung* case avoided deportation, by claiming a novel expansion of the right to family life.

The UK Borders Act 2007 should be amended, deleting Section 33(2), removing the express human rights exception and drawing a distinction between the bar on deportation to face torture or death and the bar on disruption to family life. It should replace the provision with a specific regime for handling claims that a deportee may be tortured or killed on return home. The procedure and burden of proof for establishing the risk of torture or being killed could thereby by clarified and spelt out in greater detail. The prohibition on torture and the right to life are 'non-derogable' rights under the ECHR and all the main political parties are committed to respecting them.

However, the right to respect for family life under Article 8 is a 'derogable' right and heavily qualified in the Convention itself. Article 8 itself provides:

1. Everyone has the right to respect for his private and family life, his home and his correspondence.

2. There shall be no interference by a public authority with the exercise of this right except such as is in accordance with the law and is necessary in a democratic society in the interests of national security, public safety or the economic well-being of the country, for the prevention of disorder or crime, for the protection of health or morals, or for the protection of the rights and freedoms of others.

Whilst there is no qualification on the prohibition on torture, the right to respect for family life is clearly and explicitly qualified in sub-paragraph (2), to allow deportation for the purposes of national security, law enforcement or public protection in the broadest terms. Therefore, Britain should avail itself of the 'margin of appreciation' to facilitate automatic deportation of criminals convicted of serious offences and terrorist suspects under the UK Borders Act 2007, irrespective of claims under Article 8, which are now the majority of human rights claims frustrating UK deportation proceedings. Far from undermining the ECHR, this reform would explicitly seek to give effect to Article 8(2), faithfully reflecting the intentions of the architects of the Convention which have been undermined by the Strasbourg Court.

The amendments to the Human Rights Act, recommended above, would further prevent such legislation from being surreptitiously undermined either by the UK or Strasbourg courts, because any declaration of incompatibility would revert to the government and Parliament to resolve. Elected law-makers would have the final say.

4

Reform Abroad

In addition to the domestic reforms recommended above, Britain should take advantage of its Chairmanship of the Council of Europe, between November 2011 and May 2012, to press for reform of the ECHR and the Strasbourg Court.

- **Amend the Convention regime for deportation**

The ECHR was not originally intended to restrict deportation. It is clear from Article 33 of the United Nations Refugee Convention 1951 that international human rights law in the post-war era did not envisage the restrictions on deportation that have expanded as a result of judicial legislation.

The government should consider sponsoring proposals to amend the ECHR by Protocol to reflect the distinctions drawn by the United Nations Convention Against Torture 1984 (CAT). The CAT distinguishes between torture and other forms of less serious inhuman and degrading treatment. As a result, it bars deportation to face torture but not the lesser forms of mistreatment.[64]

The Protocol could also set out in detail the approach, considered above, whereby deportation is barred where an individual faces a serious threat of being tortured or killed on return, but is permitted in relation to convicted

---

[64] Article 3.

criminals or terrorist suspects claiming rights to family life or forms of mistreatment short of torture.

The Conservative Party initiated discussions on this subject with other countries in opposition.[65] In February, the Attorney General confirmed to Parliament that wider negotiations are underway with international partners on proposals to amend the current regime under the ECHR.[66] Britain now needs to make a concerted diplomatic push to deliver reforms within the Council of Europe.

- **Focus Strasbourg on the most serious human rights abuses**

Whilst some have suggested Britain should opt out of the jurisdiction of the Strasbourg Court, whilst remaining a party to the ECHR, this would be challenging in practice.[67] It is far from clear that the other forty-six state parties would agree to such a radical split between the Convention and the Court. However, reform of the Strasbourg Court is long overdue and previous measures have been half-hearted or ineffectual.

There were six times as many applications to the Strasbourg Court in 2010 compared to 2000, with fresh claims running at over 60,000 per year.[68] The backlog of cases at the start of 2011 had reached almost 140,000 cases.

---

[65] See the speech by Baroness Neville-Jones to the Conservative Party Conference, 1 October 2008.

[66] Hansard, 10 February 2011.

[67] Michael Pinto-Duschinsky, 'Bringing Rights Back Home', Policy Exchange, 7 February 2011.

[68] See the Annual Reports of the Strasbourg Court.

These trends partly reflect the growth in internet communication and civil society strengthening access to the Court. However, it also reflects the massive widening of the Strasbourg Court's jurisdiction that has resulted from the expansion of human rights law by judicial legislation. Any international negotiations on an amending Protocol to the ECHR should therefore include measures to address the burgeoning workload of the court. The most obvious reform would be to establish clearer criteria for Strasbourg to hear cases. The International Criminal Court (ICC) operates a system known as 'complementarity', whereby the ICC only takes jurisdiction in relation to serious international crimes, leaving domestic jurisdictions to hear most cases. The ICC only steps in as a last resort, where the domestic justice system has broken down—and is either unable or unwilling to prosecute alleged war criminals. The ICC prosecutor has further focused the remit of the Court, by making clear he would only pursue cases against senior leaders responsible for the worst crimes.

An amending Protocol should follow this example, by setting criteria whereby the Strasbourg Court only intervenes as a last resort in cases to hear claims that amount to the most serious or systemic violations of rights under the ECHR. This would focus and restrain the Strasbourg Court, preventing it from engaging in judicial legislation, micro-managing domestic law-making or taking up less serious or spurious claims such as prisoner voting.

- **Introduce judicial quality control**

When reviewed in 2007, only 20 of the 45 European judges had any prior judicial experience before joining the

Strasbourg bench.[69] By 2011, the judicial calibre had not improved much: 23 out of 47 of the judges had prior judicial experience.[70]

Some of the judges are woefully lacking in experience, such as the judge for San Marino who only completed her training as a lawyer in 2002. More broadly, given the wide membership of the ECHR, many of the judges come from countries with sub-standard justice systems. Nine judges come from countries deemed not free or only partly free by Freedom House.[71] That makes it difficult for judicial candidates from those countries to establish adequate credentials to serve as an international appellate judge at the European level. Why should British cases that reach Strasbourg be subject to a lower standard of judicial scrutiny than is provided by the UK courts?

In May 2003, a panel of eminent European judges and lawyers published a report on the Strasbourg bench. The panel, which included Lord Lester and Lord Justice Sedley, criticised the 'politicised processes currently adopted in the appointment of [Strasbourg] judges', noting that 'judges selected will lack the requisite skills and abilities to discharge their duties' and warning of the 'adverse effect' on the Strasbourg Court's credibility.[72] The panel explained that nominations were frequently

---

[69] Chapter 5, *The Assault on Liberty*, 2009, by Dominic Raab.

[70] The CVs of the judges are available on the website of the Strasbourg Court.

[71] See *Freedom in the World 2011*.

[72] 'Judicial Independence: Law and Practice of Appointments to the European Court of Human Rights', *INTERIGHTS*, May 2003.

made on the basis of political loyalty, and scrutiny was influenced by party politics and diplomatic lobbying, which undermined the independence of those appointed. The net effect is 'a Court less qualified and less able to discharge its crucial mandate than it might otherwise be'.

The variable calibre of the Strasbourg judiciary is undermining the credibility and value of the Court. Proposals for an amending Protocol to the ECHR should tighten the procedure and criteria for judicial nomination and appointment, and increase transparency and accountability over the process.

5

The EU Dimension

The potential for the expansion of human rights as a result of separate developments within the European Union (EU) is beyond the scope of this paper. However, government officials and senior lawyers raised the issue during the debate on prisoner voting, suggesting that such rights might be enforceable under EU law, even if unenforceable by Strasbourg or under the Human Rights Act.[73]

The debate on prisoner voting has highlighted two specific areas where there is scope for the triplication of judicial legislation in the field of human rights law—the EU adding to problems experienced in the UK courts and Strasbourg.

First, whilst Britain's opt-out from the EU Charter of Fundamental Rights was designed to prevent creating an additional human rights jurisdiction applicable to the UK, it has yet to be properly tested in practice. The Law Society and the House of Lords EU Select Committee have commented on the legal uncertainty around the robustness of the opt-out.[74]

---

[73] See the evidence given by Aidan O'Neill QC to the House of Commons Political and Constitutional Committee, 1 February 2011.

[74] *A Guide to the Treaty of Lisbon*, Law Society, 2008; and *The Treaty of Lisbon: an impact assessment*, House of Lords EU Committee, March 2008.

Second, the EU is negotiating to become a party to the ECHR as a separate entity. It is unclear what impact this will have. There is a risk that any reforms to the Human Rights Act, ECHR and the Strasbourg Court could be undermined via the backdoor, as a result of the EU becoming a party to the Convention. The negotiations are ongoing, and Minister for Justice Jonathan Djanogly stated on 8 March 2011:

> The Government will need to be sure that any accession agreement neither enlarges the competences of the Union nor negatively affects the position of the United Kingdom and other member states in relation to the ECHR.[75]

- **Ensure EU accession to the ECHR does not increase the liabilities of the British taxpayer**

The aim of EU accession to the ECHR is to ensure EU institutions do not undermine ECHR protections. To the extent that it provides a remedy against violations by EU institutions and officials it is unobjectionable. However, the UK red-line in the negotiations—which can only reach agreement by unanimity—must be that it does not impose any additional human rights obligations or liabilities on the UK government or its taxpayers. Adding the jurisdiction of the European Court of Justice in Luxembourg over human rights in the UK would at best sow further confusion and legal uncertainty, and at worst fuel further judicial legislation from a fresh source.

---

[75] Hansard.